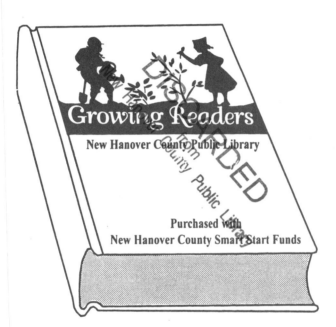

SandCastle 3

How Do You Feel?

I Feel Brave

Kelly Doudna

Published by SandCastle™, an imprint of ABDO Publishing Company, 4940 Viking Drive, Edina, Minnesota 55435.

Printed in the United States.

Photo credits: Adobe Image Library, DíAMAR, Digital Stock, PhotoDisc

Library of Congress Cataloging-in-Publication Data

Doudna, Kelly, 1963-
    I feel brave / Kelly Doudna.
      p. cm. -- (How do you feel?)
    Summary: In photographs and simple text, children tell what makes
them feel brave, such as flying high on a swing, roaring like a
lion, and knowing that they are good enough to do hard things.
     ISBN 1-57765-190-1
     1. Courage in children--Juvenile literature. [1. Courage.]
I. Title. II. Series: Doudna, Kelly, 1963- How do you feel?
BF723.C694D68 1998
152.4--dc21

                                       98-26677
                                         CIP
                                         AC

The SandCastle concept, content, and reading method have been reviewed and approved by a national advisory board including literacy specialists, librarians, elementary school teachers, early childhood education professionals, and parents.

Let Us Know

After reading the book, SandCastle would like you to tell us your stories about reading. What is your favorite page? Was there something hard that you needed help with? Share the ups and downs of learning to read. We want to hear from you! To get posted on the Abdo Publishing Company Web site, send us email at:

sandcastle@abdopub.com

About SandCastle™
Nonfiction books for the beginning reader

- Basic concepts of phonics are incorporated with integrated language methods of reading instruction. Most words are short, and phrases, letter sounds, and word sounds are repeated.

- Readability is determined by the number of words in each sentence, the number of characters in each word, and word lists based on curriculum frameworks.

- Full-color photography reinforces word meanings and concepts.

- "Words I Can Read" list at the end of each book teaches basic elements of grammar, helps the reader recognize the words in the text, and builds vocabulary.

- Reading levels are indicated by the number of flags on the castle.

Look for more SandCastle books in these three reading levels:

Level 1 (one flag)	Level 2 (two flags)	Level 3 (three flags)

Grades Pre-K to K 5 or fewer words per page	**Grades K to 1** 5 to 10 words per page	**Grades 1 to 2** 10 to 15 words per page

I feel brave when Dad
gives me a piggyback ride.

I feel brave when I pretend
I can fly like an airplane.

I feel brave when I swing
high in the air.

I feel brave when I hold my breath and swim underwater.

I feel brave when I put
my hands up and slide fast.

I feel brave when Dad
helps me do something
hard.

I feel brave when I jump into the pool.

Dad will catch me.

I feel brave when I roar like a lion to chase away bad things.

I feel brave because I know
I can do hard things.

Words I Can Read

Nouns
A noun is a person, place, or thing

air (AIR) p. 9
airplane (AIR-plane) p. 7
breath (BRETH) p. 11
Dad (DAD) pp. 5, 15, 17

lion (LYE-uhn) p. 19
pool (POOL) p. 17
ride (RIDE) p. 5

Plural Nouns
A plural noun is more than one
person, place, or thing

hands (HANDZ) p. 13

things (THINGZ) pp. 19, 21

Pronouns
A pronoun is a word that replaces a noun

I (EYE) pp. 5, 7, 9, 11, 13, 15,
17, 19, 21
me (MEE) pp. 5, 15, 17

something
(SUHM-thing) p. 15

Verbs
A verb is an action or being word

can (KAN) pp. 7, 21
catch (KACH) p. 17

chase (CHAYSS) p. 19
do (DOO) pp. 15, 21

feel (FEEL) pp. 5, 7, 9, 11, 13, 15, 17, 19, 21
fly (FLYE) p. 7
gives (GIVZ) p. 5
helps (HELPSS) p. 15
hold (HOHLD) p. 11
jump (JUHMP) p. 17
know (NOH) p. 21

pretend (pree-TEND) p. 7
put (PUT) p. 13
roar (ROR) p. 19
slide (SLIDE) p. 13
swim (SWIM) p. 11
swing (SWING) p. 9
will (WIL) p. 17

Adjectives

An adjective describes something

bad (BAD) p. 19
brave (BRAVE) pp. 5, 7, 9, 11, 13, 15, 17, 19, 21
hard (HARD) pp. 15, 21

my (MYE) pp. 11, 13
piggyback (PIG-ee-bak) p. 5

Adverbs

An adverb tells how, when, or where something happens

away (uh-WAY) p. 19
fast (FAST) p. 13
high (HYE) p. 9

underwater (uhn-dur-WAW-tur) p. 11
up (UHP) p. 13

23

Glossary

airplane - A winged machine powered by an engine.

lion - A large brown cat of Africa and southern Asia.

piggyback ride - When someone carries you on his or her shoulders or back.

pool - An area of water to swim in.